Original title:
Whimsy of the Woods

Copyright © 2025 Creative Arts Management OÜ
All rights reserved.

Author: Clara Whitfield
ISBN HARDBACK: 978-1-80567-433-7
ISBN PAPERBACK: 978-1-80567-732-1

Forest Frolics at Twilight

In the hush of dusk's embrace,
Squirrels dance with merry grace,
They wear hats made of leaves fine,
And giggle as they sip on pine.

A toad sings tunes in silly rhyme,
While owls play cards, passing time,
The fireflies wink, oh so bright,
As crickets join the mirthful night.

Beneath the trees, a fox in jest,
Juggles acorns, feeling blessed,
Each tumble brings a chuckling sound,
As laughter fills the forest ground.

The moon peeks through with a grin so wide,
A raccoon hosts the nightly ride,
On whimsical trails where shadows prance,
In this twilight fête, all creatures dance.

A Glimpse of the Sylphs

In twilight's glow, they flit and tease,
With giggles soft as summer breeze.
Their laughter floats on leaves so light,
As shadows dance and day turns night.

They hide behind the toadstools bright,
In twirls and spins, a comical sight.
With mischief true, they steal the show,
Then vanish swift, like whispers low.

Fairy Lights on Ferns

The ferns are dressed in sparkly dew,
As tiny sprites play peek-a-boo.
They juggle mushrooms, what a sight!
Sneaky flickers, glowing bright.

A gnome trips over, stumbles near,
He shakes his fist, then cracks a cheer.
For in this space, the odd fits right,
Where laughter blooms in endless night.

Breezy Antics Among the Branches

The branches sway with chuckles low,
As critters cavort, putting on a show.
Squirrels slide down, oh what a blast,
While owls hoot loud, they're having a blast.

A raccoon spins with graceful flair,
While foxes snicker from their lair.
Each gust of wind brings glee anew,
A playful world, forever askew.

The Woodland Masquerade

Beneath the boughs, a party brews,
With feathers, masks, and woodland hues.
The rabbits hop, the badgers jive,
In fuzzy suits, they come alive!

The owls preside with solemn grace,
While raccoons race to find their place.
A merry scene, with colors grand,
In this strange, enchanted wonderland.

The Squirrels' Silly Serenade

In jackets of fluff, they dance and play,
Chasing their tails in a comical way.
Nutty acrobatics in sunlight's gleam,
A chorus of giggles, a playful dream.

With acorns in paws, they strut about,
Chattering nonsense, they sing and shout.
A squirrelly tune fills the twinkling air,
As branches sway gently, without a care.

Gossamer Dreams Among the Pines

Between the tall trees, a laughter flows,
In far-off lands where the magic grows.
Gossamer creatures weave tales so bright,
Spinning their webs in the shimmering light.

With twinkling eyes and a swirl of dust,
They dance on the breeze, they leap and trust.
Whirlwinds of giggles, they twirl and glide,
As secrets of joy in the shadows bide.

Whispers in the Willow

Beneath the fringe of a willow's dress,
Whispers arise, a playful mess.
Breezes tickle, the branches sway,
As leaves play hide and seek all day.

A squirrel peeks out, a wink and a grin,
Soft chuckles echo, the fun begins.
With shadows that dance on the cool, green floor,
The giggles of nature, we simply adore.

Fancies on Ferns

On velvet green ferns, the fairies prance,
In puddles of sunlight, they skip and dance.
With petals for hats and wings made of light,
They twirl like confetti, oh what a sight!

Silly little sprites in a leafy parade,
With jokes in the air, their laughter displayed.
In a world of green hugs, where fun is the rule,
They sprinkle their magic, so joyful, so cool.

Curious Creatures In Their Nooks

In a hollow tree, a squirrel peeks,
With a tiny hat, he often speaks.
Chasing his tail on a windy day,
He giggles loudly, then rolls away.

A hedgehog snorts with a tiny grin,
Searching for snacks that are stuffed within.
He juggles acorns, trying too hard,
While a grumpy owl lets down a guard.

A rabbit hops with a silly gait,
Her shoes too big, oh what a fate!
Laughing out loud, they twirl and prance,
In the dappled light, they take a chance.

Each nook is filled with laughter's cheer,
As the creatures gather, full of good cheer.
With tiny hats and shoes that squeak,
The woodland's joy is far from bleak.

The Secret Lives of Twigs

Twigs wear capes in the autumn breeze,
Whispering secrets to all of the trees.
They dance a jig when no one can see,
With ants as their guests, sipping sweet tea.

A twig dressed as a knight joins the fray,
Chasing tiny bugs that wander away.
In battles of leaves, they swing and sway,
Making a ruckus, then sneak out to play.

One sneaky stick, with a twisted grin,
Pretends it's a snake, causing a spin.
While bees take bets on who'll win the race,
As they zoom around, quickening the pace.

In moonlit moments, these twigs all sing,
About the adventures that night would bring.
Surrounded by laughter, they sway with style,
These unassuming sticks know how to smile.

A Chant from the Charmed Grove

In the heart of the grove, a chorus chimes,
With chirps and giggles, they mix their rhymes.
Frogs croak loudly, while crickets tap dance,
Every odd creature joins in for a chance.

A raccoon rolls around, wearing a mask,
Singing a tune, it's a curious task.
In twilight's glow, they share silly lore,
About the moon's cheese and the stars galore.

A bumblebee buzzing, quite out of tune,
Dances in circles beneath the full moon.
While a shy little mouse plays the flute,
With a toe-tapping beat that none can refute.

As they chant and chuckle, the night feels bright,
With a sprinkle of magic in pure delight.
The grove knows secrets, and laughter ignites,
In this silly gathering of whimsical sights.

Bouncing Shadows on the Trail

Up and down, the shadows play,
Bouncing around in a merry way.
A fox tiptoes with a playful grin,
While jumpy shadows fetch him in.

A deer leaps high like a starry sprite,
Chasing shadows that dance in the night.
With giggles echoing through rustling leaves,
Twirling and whirling, the night deceives.

Across the path, a shadow winks,
Making the rabbits giggle and rinks.
Each step they take is a joyful cheer,
As if the moon has lent them a gear.

In the woodland's heart, where silliness reigns,
Bouncing shadows cure all the pains.
Under the rays of a soft, silver veil,
All are enchanted on the winding trail.

Bouncing Butterflies in the Glade

In the meadow, they twirl and spin,
Wings like candy, bright and thin.
A hop, a skip, they flirt and tease,
Tickling flowers, dancing with ease.

They giggle as they chase the breeze,
Playing tag with playful trees.
Each flicker brings a happy sigh,
As they leap to the azure sky.

Joyful Jingles from the Thicket

The branches sway, a merry tune,
Squirrels dance beneath the moon.
With tiny bells, they jingle and jive,
Atop the boughs, the critters thrive.

Rabbits hop with hats so wide,
Wearing smiles, they take a ride.
The thicket hums with laughter bright,
As shadows play and hearts take flight.

A Tangle of Wishes and Whispers

In a corner where secrets lie,
Dreams tumble out, like birds that fly.
Whispers twirl on a dandelion,
Imagination's tiny lion.

Each wish is dressed in colors bold,
Twinkling tales of adventures told.
They twist and turn in the gentle air,
Floating softly, without a care.

Capers of the Cattails

Down by the pond, the cattails sway,
Marsh frogs joke and leap in play.
With silly hats made from reeds,
They laugh and prance, fulfilling needs.

Dragonflies zoom, they're racing fast,
In silly patterns, they're built to last.
A splash, a splash, the water flies,
And all around, the chorus cries.

Tweets and Treetops

In treetops high, the birds all sing,
Tales of mischief that makes hearts spring.
Squirrels dart with acorn delight,
Planning parties by moon's soft light.

A crow in shades, with a top hat fine,
Tells silly jokes over cups of brine.
The forest giggles, a playful tease,
As rabbits dance with the rustling leaves.

Gossamer Threads of Time

Through the glen, a spider weaves,
Stories of laughter among the leaves.
Wisps of light twirl and glide,
As frogs in bow ties take a ride.

The clock ticks loud, but not too fast,
In this realm, the die is cast.
A chipmunk's grin, a sneaky wink,
Time plays tricks—just stop and think!

The Curious Paths of Padded Feet

Tiny paws on a winding trail,
Chasing shadows with a tiny wail.
The mushrooms giggle, all in a row,
As hedgehogs tiptoe, moving slow.

A raccoon's hat, oh what a sight,
Makes even the owls chuckle at night.
The path grows twisted, a puzzle game,
Each step a riddle, all feel the same.

Echoes of the Elusive Glade

In the glade where secrets rest,
A whisper floats, a feathered jest.
Mice in a meeting, all dressed in style,
Debating cheese with a giggling smile.

Moonbeams chuckle, casting hues,
As dancing flowers exchange their news.
The air is sweet with laughter's sigh,
In this hidden place where joys comply.

Whirlwinds of Wonder

In the heart of the twirling trees,
A squirrel skates on a gentle breeze.
He pirouettes on a mushroom chair,
Chasing shadows without a care.

The bunnies giggle, a soft ballet,
Their cotton tails leading the way.
With each hop, a sprinkle of cheer,
They dance in circles, drawing near.

A mischievous crow steals a cap,
Wearing it proudly, setting a trap.
He caws a tune, a jolly jest,
In this merry realm, he's quite the guest.

A dandelion, with a wink so bright,
Blows its seeds into the light.
They float like dreams on a golden stream,
In this world of giggles, life's a dream.

Mischief in the Meadow

In a meadow full of bounce,
Grass blades sway like dancers prounce.
A ladybug, with spots of red,
Plays hide and seek in garden bed.

A fox with a hat, a cheeky sight,
Sneaks up on snails with all his might.
They curl in their shells with squeaks of glee,
As he dances away, full of spree.

Butterflies swing on a breeze so sweet,
Chasing the ants in a skipping feat.
With every flutter, a giggling cheer,
Nature's mischief is ever near.

In this meadow of laughter we roam,
Every creature calls it home.
With each chuckle and every sigh,
Nature's lightheartedness fills the sky.

Lurking Laughter of the Larks

High in the branches, the larks do sing,
Their notes twirl like a playful string.
With feathers ruffled and heads held high,
They giggle at clouds floating by.

A curious owl blinks in surprise,
As squirrels practice acrobatic flies.
They tumble and twirl, a chaotic scene,
Making up for the acorns unseen.

The hedgehog rolls, a spiky ball,
Chasing shadows, he is enthralled.
With a puff and a chuckle, he leaps with flair,
In this vibrant theater, no one can stare.

The sun dips low, casting fun little beams,
Illuminating their giggling dreams.
A tapestry woven with joy and delight,
In this nature's stage, the laughter is bright.

Flirting with Florals

Petals chatter in the morning glow,
Flirting softly, whispering low.
The daisies pick dresses, all in a row,
Preparing for parties they all know.

A bee does a jig, all busy and neat,
Buzzing along to a vibrant beat.
With pollen as confetti, he throws it wide,
Creating a party where blooms confide.

Roses and tulips tease in the sun,
Chasing the butterflies, oh what fun!
They sway and they twirl, in frolicsome glee,
Reminding the world just how free they can be.

As twilight beckons, the evening speaks,
The flowers settle, their laughter peaks.
In a world of colors, here chaos reigns,
Where nature's charm forever remains.

The Mirth of the Melodic Meadow.

In the field where flowers sway,
A frog dons a hat of hay.
He croaks a tune, a jolly tune,
While bees tap dance beneath the moon.

The squirrels juggle acorns high,
As butterflies flutter by.
A rabbit laughs, a puppet show,
As raindrops tap with a cheerful flow.

Enchanted Glades

In the shade where shadows play,
A fox decides to paint all day.
With strokes of green and dabs of blue,
He laughs at trees that dance askew.

The owls gossip, what a sight,
As raccoons bicker, claiming right.
The sun peeks in with a cheeky wink,
They stop to stare, not a clue to think.

Secrets of the Sylvan

Among the leaves, the secrets spill,
A chipmunk's got a hidden thrill.
He tells of tales from branches high,
Of grand adventures in the sky.

With whispers soft, the trees conspire,
To build a swing from nature's fire.
So come and play where laughter glows,
In tangled vines where mischief flows.

Dance of the Dappled Light

In sunlight's dance, the shadows twirl,
A bashful snail begins to whirl.
With a twist and turn, oh what a show,
He scoffs at time, so nice and slow.

The grasshoppers join in the fun,
With hops and skips, they love to run.
And if you listen, you'll surely hear,
A cheerful tune from the trees so near.

Whirling Petals of Joy

In the breeze, petals twirl,
They wear tiny crowns, what a swirl!
Each landing spot, a giggle loud,
Nature's jesters, so proud.

Dancing under the cheeky sun,
Flower fairies leap, oh what fun!
In petals' flight, laughter springs,
A parade of joy on delicate wings.

Bumblebees buzzing with glee,
Join the party, carelessly free.
Tiptoeing through blooms, make a fuss,
In this garden, there's room for us.

A butterfly chuckles, wings so bright,
Winks at the bushes, what a sight!
With every flap, they tease the air,
Nature's humor is everywhere.

Laughing Leaves in the Loom

Leaves chatter softly, huddled tight,
Tickling each other, pure delight.
In the loom of branches, tales unfold,
Whispers of joy, both gentle and bold.

Squirrels with cheeky acrobatics swing,
Grabbing the air, like it's a string.
In their mischief, giggles arise,
Nature's jesters in disguise.

A leaf drops down with a playful grin,
"Catch me if you can!" it doth begin.
Rustling laughter in shades of green,
Tickling the ground where they have been.

Through the twinkling trees, joy spreads wide,
Laughter echoes, no need to hide.
In every rustle, a spark of cheer,
Nature's humor, always near.

The Secret Society of Saplings

Tiny trunks form a giddy line,
Whispering secrets, so divine.
With roots entwined, they plot and scheme,
In their leafy world, they dare to dream.

A conspiracy of sprigs, oh so sly,
Bringing smiles as they reach for the sky.
Playing peek-a-boo with passing deer,
In their little group, there's never fear.

Tall tales exchanged, both silly and sweet,
Every belly laugh, a leafy treat.
Under the starlight, they giggle and sway,
In their secret world, they dance and play.

The moon winks down, a knowing friend,
To the cheerful saplings, laughter won't end.
In the wild, they find joy anew,
Their little pranks, forever true.

Disguised Delights of Dusk

As twilight slips on its shimmering cloak,
The shadows giggle, the night awoke.
Mice in capes, ready for fun,
They scamper about, never done.

Crickets chirp in a silly tone,
Playing music, they joyfully own.
Each note a chuckle, laughter begins,
In the dark, a surprise that spins.

Fireflies blink, a dance of flicks,
Lighting up the world with little tricks.
They flicker like stars, mischievous and bright,
Guiding the giggles of the night.

Behind the trees, whispers abound,
With every rustle, joy can be found.
In this playful evening, hearts collide,
Under the moonlight, let laughter abide.

Squirrelly Serenades

Nutty dancers in the trees,
Chasing shadows on the breeze.
With acorn hats and tiny shoes,
They sing their songs and dance their blues.

Pinecone drums and leafy flutes,
Squirrels sway in furry suits.
Jumps and flips, they twist and twirl,
While giggles float in nature's whirl.

From branch to branch they leap with cheer,
Comedic acts that bring us near.
Tiny jesters, bold and spry,
Underneath the laughing sky.

In the woodland, all is bright,
Squirrelly serenades delight.
Round they go, with silly glee,
A forest show, just wait and see!

Whispers in the Wilderness

A rabbit wears a bowtie fine,
He teases birds with jokes divine.
The trees confide in rustling tones,
As critters share their silly bones.

Badgers crack a mystery case,
While foxes prance with witty grace.
The air is filled with chuckles bright,
As whispers dance from night to light.

Wily owls, with glinting eyes,
Join in on all the clever lies.
With laughter echoing like a tune,
The woods are alive with fun so strewn.

Each secret shared, a little jest,
In nature's arms, we're truly blessed.
A wilderness of giggles play,
In the daytime and at dusk's ballet.

The Jester's Grove

In a grove where laughter flows,
Gnomes wear shoes that honk and pose.
With rainbow wigs and painted cheeks,
They crack up those who take a peek.

Frogs in crowns, with manners odd,
Dance about, give leaps a nod.
Through twisted vines, their antics spread,
While butterflies snicker overhead.

Jokes are told from tree to tree,
Making mushrooms giggle with glee.
In this realm of playful sound,
The jester's magic knows no bound.

As twilight paints the meadow gold,
The silent trees chime in, all bold.
With every chuckle, the night ignites,
In the jester's grove, pure delight!

Fantastic Flights of Fancy

Bumblebees in tiny hats,
Buzzing tales of acrobats.
While butterflies in gowns so bright,
Twirl and glide, a joyful sight.

With rainbow kites made of leaves,
The critters play, as life deceives.
A ladybug, the queen of fun,
Commands the skies till day is done.

Owl with spectacles so round,
Shares his wisdom, laughter-bound.
As fawns spin in the golden light,
Each twist and turn, pure joy in flight.

In this realm of frolic free,
The air is full of jubilee.
Fantastic flights where dreams grow wide,
A fanciful ride on nature's tide!

Chasing Shadows Through the Clearing

In dappled light, the shadows play,
A squirrel wearing stripes, hip-hip hooray!
He giggles as he leaps, what a sight,
Twisting through the leaves, oh what delight!

The sun peeks in through branches wide,
Where laughter dances, glee can't hide.
A toad, with hat, sings tunes so bright,
As flowers sway to the song of the light.

Under broad oaks, the rabbits prance,
In their tiny shoes, they twirl and dance.
With every hop, the mushrooms bob,
Cheering along, just join the mob!

The breeze is cheeky, tickling all,
As nature hosts a merry call.
So come along and feel the cheer,
In the clearing where shadows appear!

Mirthful Whispers of the Wild

The bumblebee dons a tiny hat,
Buzzing past with a chuckle and chat.
A flower winks with petals aglow,
As butterflies gossip, fluttering slow.

The brook giggles over stones so smooth,
Whispering secrets in a playful groove.
A bear in pajamas, what a sight,
Dances through branches, pure delight!

The moon peeked in, with a grin so wide,
And joined the creatures for the wild ride.
A fox cracked jokes; the night echoed laughter,
In this enchanted forest, ever after.

The nightingale croons a silly tune,
As shadows waltz beneath the moon.
In the wild, where spirits instill,
Joy multiplies, a dance at will!

The Riddle of the Rustling Vines

A twisty vine had words to share,
It tickled the trees, filling the air.
"Why do owls sleep, when it's dark?"
"Cause up in the sky, they're the spark!"

The wise old owl perched high and proud,
Chortling softly, he'd sing aloud.
As leaves danced by, the riddle swelled,
In nature's game, each secret held.

A hedgehog pondered, scratching his chin,
"What makes the sun wear a crescent grin?"
The vines giggled, teasing the breeze,
A puzzle exists, with nature, we tease!

The forest chuckled, green and spry,
With antics shared, they reached for the sky.
Together they laughed, one riddle at a time,
In this joyful grove, life is a rhyme!

Skylarks Over Misty Lanes

Skylarks soar on a humor high,
Witty songs echo as they fly.
One fluffs his feathers, spry and bold,
Sharing tales of mischief, funny and old.

The cobwebs sway in a rhythmic grace,
A wizard's hat and a jolly face.
The rabbits chuckle at the scene,
A party of critters, all in between.

"Why did the bush start to wiggle and dance?"
"Because it spied a flower glance!"
They giggle with glee under mists so light,
In lanes of laughter, all feels right.

As dawn paints the sky, fresh and new,
Each creature knows what they must do.
Join in the fun, let worries release,
In the heart of the morn, find sweet peace!

Laughter Among the Leaves

Squirrels in hats, so bright and grand,
Swinging on branches, a merry band.
Acorns as snacks, they toss in the air,
   Chasing the wind without a care.

Frogs leap in rhythm, a dance so spry,
  To the owl's hoot, they leap and fly.
  Rabbits in bowties join with a grin,
As laughter rings out, where fun begins.

A raccoon with glasses reads from a book,
  While beetles gather for a croaking look.
  Every rustle and giggle, a jolly event,
In the heart of the forest, time's merriment.

So join the parade as it tramples the ground,
Where absurdity flourishes and joy abounds.
  Nature's ensemble with quirks to behold,
  In this land of delight, where stories unfold.

Echoes of the Elfin Realm

In the glen where the giggles play,
Tiny folk with mischief sway.
Whispers and chuckles echo so clear,
As they scribe their pranks with a sprinkle of cheer.

Pixies with wings painted in hues,
Plotting their tricks with theatrical views.
They tug at your shoelace, then vanish with glee,
Leaving behind a perplexed plea.

Grasshoppers strum on an acorn bass,
As the fireflies waltz in a luminous race.
Mushrooms stand tall, wearing caps of bright red,
While the moonlight giggles, spinning tales in their head.

Under the stars, the mischief unfolds,
As elfin laughter in the nighttime molds.
A world of wonders, where folly writes,
In the echoes of magic, where joy ignites.

Sunbeams Tangle in Twigs

Sunbeams tumble, a bright golden shout,
  Twirling with leaves, giggling about.
  Branches twist up in a bowing spree,
    As shadows dance with glee at tea.

A warbler hops, with a wink and a smile,
  Juggling its worms in a most silly style.
While daises wear crowns made of sunlight,
  The bloom of laughter fills day and night.

In this playful glen where the breezes tease,
  A snail dons a vest that flaps in the breeze.
  Tiny creatures hosting a grand ball affair,
    With acorn hats and fine feathered wear.

So swirl with the sunlight, let whimsy ignite,
In a world where the tangles are pure delight.
Through twigs and beams, joy sparkles anew,
  In this playful place, with the skies so blue.

Tales from the Timberland

Bears in pajamas share bedtime tales,
While raccoons toast marshmallows, a feast that prevails.
Foxes with laughter weave stories of old,
In a woodland theater, where wonders unfold.

Chipmunks in capes run swift through the brush,
Chasing bright butterflies in a wild little rush.
They spin silly yarns of their frolicsome days,
While the trees listen in with rustling praise.

Owls wearing spectacles tell jokes on the fly,
Tickling the moonbeams as they drift by.
Each twig's a witness to their jovial spree,
In the timberland tales of pure jubilee.

So gather around for a whimsical night,
Where laughter and stories take sudden flight.
In the heart of the forest, let joyful words blend,
For in every tale, the fun has no end.

Mysteries Beneath the Canopy

A squirrel wears a tiny hat,
He claims it's for his birthday brat.
The mushrooms giggle in delight,
As shadows dance in the soft twilight.

A wise old owl has lost his specs,
He squints and gets the wrong text.
The trees lean in to share a tale,
Of fairies riding on a snail.

A rabbit juggles with some nuts,
While hedgehogs laugh in little huts.
The parrot squawks a riddle loud,
As butterflies flit 'round a cloud.

Little gnomes with paintbrushes bright,
Turn acorns into disco lights.
They party hard, the forest groans,
And tree trunks sway like wobbling tones.

Frolic in the Foliage

In leafy greens, the critters prance,
They waltz around in a merry dance.
With sticky vines as their ballet stage,
The forest floor becomes a page.

A brazen fox in polka dots,
Steals cookies from the forest pots.
The elves all giggle, throw confetti,
As thunder shakes, they shout, 'How petty!'

Amidst the ferns, a turtle spins,
While mice cheer on with tiny grins.
A beetle leads a conga line,
With acorn hats, they all look fine.

As day turns dusk, a lantern glows,
Porcupines dance in crazy rows.
They celebrate the day's grand feats,
With joyful hops on furry feet.

The Playful Breeze

A gentle gust tickles the trees,
It carries off the bumblebees.
They buzz around with silly flair,
While crickets giggle in mid-air.

Leaves twirl down like confetti bright,
Chasing shadows through the night.
A cheeky crow steals a sunhat,
As frogs croak jokes beneath the mat.

A dancing branch waves at the sky,
It beckons clouds and birds that fly.
The wind whispers secrets of glee,
While critters chuckle in harmony.

The breeze invites the stars to peek,
As moonlight spills with playful cheek.
In the rustling grass, we all unite,
With laughter echoing through the night.

Bubbles in the Brook

Bubbles rise in the bubbling brook,
Where fish wear boots and fairies cook.
A waterfall sings a splishy song,
While dragonflies zip and whirl along.

The toads play leapfrog, take a chance,
Each splash sends ripples in a dance.
Turtles float like tiny boats,
Chasing shadows with silly coats.

A frog plays chess with a tiny snail,
While a catfish shares an old tall tale.
The bubbles giggle, pop and burst,
As water nymphs quench their thirst.

At sunset's glow, the water shimmers,
And so the brook continues to glimmer.
With laughter echoing night and day,
In this bubble bath where critters play.

Breeze-Bound Frolics

A squirrel did a jig on a branch so high,
With acorns in tow, he danced in the sky.
The leaves all giggled as they swayed in delight,
While crickets composed a tune for the night.

Beneath the tall oaks, a rabbit did hop,
Wearing a hat made of soft thistle top.
He twirled with a heron, oh what a sight!
A band of the wild, under stars shining bright.

A fox in a waistcoat, quite dapper and neat,
Told stories of squirrels and their summer retreat.
His pals laughed in echo, with voices so bold,
As they rolled on the grass, all merry and gold.

Under a moonbeam, the fireflies played,
Their tiny bright lanterns glimmering displayed.
Amidst all the sillies, the night carried on,
With the breeze as a partner, till the dawn had drawn.

Dance of the Dappled Shadows

In the glen where the shadows come out to prance,
A beetle in top hat led the grand dance.
The daisies were twirling in skirts of pure white,
While mushrooms trumpeted, 'Join us tonight!'

A hedgehog on stilts wobbled to and fro,
Bumping into boulders, but loving the show.
The moon cast a grin, brightening the scene,
As frogs croaked their rhythm, a grand serenade keen.

The grasshoppers giggled, up high they took flight,
In herky-jerky leaps, they brightened the night.
The dance was contagious, horizon to trees,
Making even the owls nod along with the breeze.

With whimsy contagious, the forest took cheer,
As whispers of laughter danced soft in the ear.
Each creature enchanted, with hearts full of song,
All joined in the revels, where merriment thronged.

Sylvan Surprises

A raccoon in pajamas peeked out from the moss,
Claiming he'd found the world's biggest loss.
It turned out to be a lost shoe so sleek,
Which he wore on his head, looking trendy and chic.

An owl with glasses surveyed all below,
Taking notes on the antics that started to flow.
He chuckled as critters misstepped in their play,
Wondering who'd trip in a most comical way.

The stream had a bubble that looked like a mouse,
Causing giggles and glances from each tiny house.
A frog leaped beside it, quite sure of his stake,
Announcing the launch of the first bubble bake!

The trees joined the mischief, swaying to and fro,
As breezes caught whispers from roots down below.
With laughter and surprises, the night spun around,
In the heart of the forest, where joy can be found.

Fables Among the Foliage

A wise old raccoon claimed he once saw a ghost,
Who danced in the twilight and made the most boast.
With a flick of his tail, he spun tales that would thrill,
Yet turned out to be just a colorful quill.

A cricket wrote poetry beneath a bright star,
Chirping out sonnets of journeys afar.
His friends gathered 'round, enrapt in his verse,
As bugs in the night took turns to rehearse.

A bear with a bowtie declared it was time,
To host a grand tale-swap with snacks—how sublime!
With honey and berries, they feasted galore,
Trading stories and giggles till nobody could snore.

So fables arose in the twilight's soft gleam,
Of unlikely heroes and a wide, wondrous dream.
In the foliage's cradle, joy scattered like seeds,
As laughter was woven through imagination's reeds.

Chronicles of the Cuckoo's Nest

In a tree with a view, the cuckoo took flight,
Wearing mismatched socks, oh what a sight!
Squirrels giggled and butterflies danced,
Every feathered friend, in laughter, pranced.

A raccoon tried singing, but lost all his tunes,
While a wise old owl grinned under the moon.
A rabbit juggled berries, red and round,
As the laughter echoed through the leafy surround.

The frog on his lily pad croaked out a jest,
While a snail in a cape thought he was the best.
"Slow and steady wins the amusing race!"
They cheered for the critter with a slippery pace.

So come join the party — oh what a spree!
In the cuckoo's nest, all are wild and free.
With jokes and with jests, they craftily play,
In this quirky abode, it's a funny ballet.

Frolics in the Ferny Forge

Where the green ferns giggle and the mushrooms sway,
A band of odd creatures frolic and play.
The pixies throw sparkles, a giggling parade,
While a grumpy old gnome watches, dismayed.

A cat perched on a hedgehog, what a sight to behold,
With tales of adventure begging to be told.
Bumblebees buzzing in mismatched hats,
Turn a dull day into fun-loving chats.

Dancing among daisies, the critters unite,
A weasel in slippers, oh what a delight!
Their laughter spills over the brook's gentle hum,
In the heart of this forge, the fun is not dumb.

They spin silly stories, weave tales of the grand,
In this fern-kissed haven, a whimsical band.
So join in the fun, don't be shy or forlorn,
In the frolicsome ferns, new joys are reborn.

Secrets of the Songbird's Retreat

In the nook of the tree, where the songbirds conspire,
They share little secrets that sparkles inspire.
A finch fluffed like popcorn with tales to unveil,
While the sparrow spun stories, of a very tall snail.

A parrot juggling nuts, with flair and with grace,
Finds feathers in places, not meant for their place.
A chatty chickadee, with a wink and a nod,
Spread giggles and whispers of a clever façade.

They chirp about mischief, a squirrel in a dress,
And the time that a fox tried to pick up a mess.
With each note they warble, the giggles surround,
In this retreat of the songbirds, pure laughter is found.

So come hear the tales, let your heart take to wing,
With melodies shared, and the joy that they bring.
In the secrets of songbirds, frivolity thrives,
As laughter takes flight and the humor arrives.

Journey Through the Jumbled Roots

Amidst tangled thickets, where nobody knows,
A rabbit sports goggles and glows in his pose.
Worms take up tango, beneath the warm light,
As the owls on the branches chuckle at sight.

A hedgehog on roller skates quickly goes by,
With a crowd of amazed bugs all waving goodbye.
The ants toss confetti in glee on the ground,
In this jumbled nook, the fun knows no bound.

The mushrooms erupt, with colors so bright,
Each toadstool a hat, a delightful sight.
"Who needs a map?" chirped a bird with a grin,
As they danced through the roots beside the old bin.

So wander this path, let your giggles abound,
In the jumbled roots, hilarity's found.
A journey of laughter, where all can partake,
In the wilderness wild, where the silly awake.

Pitter-Patter of Curious Feet

Tiny paws and fluttering wings,
Laughter echoes, the forest sings.
Squirrels wear hats, all so bright,
While the rabbits hop with glee and delight.

Mice dance in shoes, oh what a sight,
Chasing their tails in the soft moonlight.
A hedgehog giggles, tries to run fast,
But rolls in a tumble, oh, what a blast!

Under the mushrooms, shadows do play,
Chasing the edges of the light of day.
Each pitter-patter, a joyful cheer,
In nature's playground, everyone's near.

Can you hear the chatter, the rustling leaves?
The woodland creatures pull up their sleeves.
A parade of laughter, a playful retreat,
Making mischief with each little beat.

The Jolly Jamboree

A raccoon with spoons starts to tap,
While owls in top hats begin to clap.
The frogs croak a tune, quite out of scale,
As fireflies twinkle and giggle without fail.

Ants in a line, like a conga, they sway,
Join the festivity, hip-hip-hooray!
With acorns confetti, they dance round a tree,
While butterflies flutter, wild and free.

The big bear sneezes, the whole crowd takes flight,
Spinning in circles, what a hilarious sight!
As laughter erupts from the leaves up high,
Beneath the star blanket, with a twinkle in the sky.

Oh, what a jolly, uproarious night,
In this woodland fiesta, everything's bright.
So gather your friends for a marvelous spree,
At the merry jamboree, come sing with glee!

A Canopied Carnival

Beneath the green canopy, the fun begins,
The critters all gather, all losses turn wins.
A fox juggles berries, a sight quite absurd,
While the owl announces with a giggle, unheard.

The raccoons play games, hiding behind trees,
Launching acorns like rockets, oh, what a tease!
Chasing their shadows, they twist and they shout,
While the wise old turtle just meanders about.

With laughter contagious, and joy in the air,
A party erupts; you can't help but stare.
The deer prance in circles, all lit up like stars,
As the squirrels trade stories of adventures near and far.

Dresses of leaves, hats made of twigs,
This carnival of cheer, oh, it surely digs.
Come join the fables, sing loud and true,
In the heart of the forest, there's fun waiting for you!

Fanciful Footprints in the Forest

Little paw prints on a path of delight,
Follow the giggles, dance into the night.
A parade of critters, in costume they flow,
Every step sprinkled with a shimmering glow.

Frolicsome bear in a tutu so bright,
While chipmunks make music, oh, what a sight!
Chasing the shadows, they scamper and play,
Swaying to rhythms, oh, hip-hip-hooray!

See how the pathways twist and they twirl,
The forest is bustling, a magical whirl.
With whimsical prints leading hearts to explore,
The charmed woodland invites forevermore.

Among the tall trees, where sunbeams peek,
The joyful footprints are all unique.
So laugh and discover, let your spirits roam,
In this fanciful land, you'll feel right at home.

Mirth Among the Maple Boughs

In the shade where shadows play,
Squirrels danced, they laughed away.
Nutty jokes, they'd share in glee,
While bunnies hopped around the tree.

Maples giggled in the breeze,
Tickling leaves, oh what a tease!
A parrot sang a silly tune,
As raccoons danced beneath the moon.

Frogs found hats, quite spiffy too,
To join the fun, as frogs will do.
The party swayed, to unseen beats,
With every thump of tiny feet.

A tickle fight, the air did fill,
As butterflies swirled, up on the hill.
Laughter rang, a joyful sound,
In the heart of nature, pure frolic found.

The Sprightly Sprite's Adventure

A sprite flew high on sparkling wings,
With mischief plans and funny things.
She sprinkled dreams on foxtails bright,
   Creating giggles deep into night.

She tripped on mushrooms, bounced in glee,
   Turned a fog into a swimming sea.
With pixie dust, she made a cake,
And soon the forest started to shake.

Toadstools laughed and willow sighed,
As hedgehogs danced, oh what a ride!
The sprite wore shoes of rainbow hues,
And juggled acorns, a sight to amuse.

At sunset's glow, she took her bow,
The laughter faded, whispers of wow!
But stay tuned friends, for another day,
   When sprites return to laugh and play.

Revelry in the Reeds

The reeds held secrets, soft and sweet,
Where crickets chirped a catchy beat.
With dancing fireflies all aglow,
They started a party in the meadow.

A frog in a bowtie, quite absurd,
Recited poems, oh how they stirred!
A dragonfly spun with dizzy flair,
While turtles giggled without a care.

The moon took notes from every jest,
As reeds whispered clues in a jovial fest.
With weedy hats, the creatures cheered,
A celebration that all revered.

Oh, how the laughter lit the night,
As friends united in pure delight.
They promised more when the stars would gleam,
In hidden nooks, where joy is the theme.

Treetop Lullabies

Up in the branches, a tune took flight,
With koalas singing soft and light.
A sloth strummed low on a leafy harp,
As night critters joined with a chirpy sharp.

The owls wore glasses, quite a sight!
A croaking chorus filled the night.
They played with shadows, danced with glee,
Hooting echoes of harmony.

The raccoons clapped with paws so keen,
Creating rhythms, a joyful scene.
With every note, the tree did sway,
As dreams took flight, all night they'd play.

At dawn's first light, the music ceased,
But laughter lingered, joy released.
Treetop tales and melodies,
Would fill their hearts with sweet memories.

Giggling Glimmers in the Gloom

Under mushrooms, laughter hides,
Squirrels dance with wild-eyed pride.
Raccoons play tricks behind the trunks,
While owls giggle, thinking 'punks!'

Moonbeams tickle leaves so bright,
Bats flip-flop in the night.
Fireflies wear their shiny hats,
As trees gossip with friendly chats.

A hedgehog's laugh, a sneaky squeak,
Makes the very tall trees peak.
With every rustle, giggles grow,
The forest's joy in ebb and flow.

As dawn approaches, snickers fade,
But memories linger, a playful braid.
Tomorrow's mischief is on its way,
In the glimmers where the creatures play.

The Fable of the Fern Fronds

In a glade of vibrant green,
Ferns exchanged a cheeky scene.
"I'm taller!" one did proudly boast,
While others giggled, playing host.

A bunny hopped, a cheeky sprite,
Dared the ferns to dance in light.
With twirls and twists, they started prance,
Creating quite the leafy dance.

A parrot perched above the fray,
Cawed out jokes in funny play.
"Why did the fern cross the brook?
To see how pretty it could look!"

The laughter roared through leafy glades,
As friendships blossomed in shy shades.
A fable told, in whispers soft,
Of fronds and fun that wafted aloft.

Curious Knots and Twists

Tangled roots like snickering vines,
Winding stories, hilarious signs.
A squirrel got lost in a leafy maze,
Chasing his tail in a comical daze.

A brooding toad croaked a rhyme,
While ladybugs joked about the time.
"Who can guess where the wind may blow?
Just follow the giggles, go with the flow!"

Knots of laughter, twists of glee,
In every nook, a jubilee.
A fox rolled over in soft, warm grass,
While fireflies flashed as if to pass.

Twilight drew laughter out of sight,
As shadows danced in playful flight.
Yet in the dark, giggles linger,
Curious knots tied by nature's finger.

Swaying Stars in the Understory

Beneath the trees, stars twinkle wide,
But here on earth, the giggles glide.
With mushrooms as seats, the critters sing,
To the rhythm of the forest's zing.

Crickets chirp in a silly tune,
While raccoons mimic the smiling moon.
"Hey, what's up?" they cheerfully chime,
"To dance or nap? It's the perfect time!"

A hedgehog arranges acorn caps,
As laughter erupts from tiny chaps.
In the shade, they bounce and sway,
Creating mischief in their own way.

Stars peek lower, in colors grand,
As sprites toss giggles across the land.
In the understory, joy takes flight,
While all the creatures play all night.

Enchanted Canopy

Squirrels in hats play games of chase,
With acorns flying through the space.
A rabbit sings a silly tune,
While dancing 'neath the laughing moon.

Trees chuckle low, their branches sway,
As critters frolic, come what may.
A fox in socks prances with glee,
In this woodland jubilee!

A parrot tells jokes; the owl can't sleep,
As fireflies twinkle, secrets they keep.
The shadows shift, they play hide and seek,
In a world where laughter is unique.

Mushrooms giggle, all plump and round,
Telling tales of the fun they've found.
The breeze carries whispers, a cheeky breeze,
In our enchanted leafy trees.

Secrets Beneath the Ferns

Beneath the ferns, the critters conspire,
With whispers and giggles that never tire.
A snail in a bowtie slips on the dew,
While a hedgehog waltzes, oh so askew!

A raccoon with marbles starts to play ball,
In a game where no one cares if they fall.
The mushrooms join in, a scurry of feet,
With laughter that echoes—what a funny feat!

Ladybugs dance on a leaf so wide,
While gophers race, their cheeks filled with pride.
The dandelions cheer with a fluttering grin,
In this hidden nook, where fun starts to spin.

Each secret shared is wrapped in delight,
In a world where every day feels just right.
Under the ferns, where laughter is deep,
Magic unfolds in tiny leaps!

Lullabies of Leafy Laughter

A chorus of crickets hums through the night,
As the owls join along in a friendly fright.
Beneath swaying branches, the stars twinkle bright,
While raccoons hold concerts, a delightful sight!

The breeze carries laughter, soft as a kiss,
As chipmunks tell tales no one can miss.
The soft lullabies float through the trees,
Bringing smiles and giggles that dance in the breeze.

The fireflies twirl, like lights in a show,
While frogs croak their verses, a rhythmic flow.
Each leaf holds a secret, a joke or a pun,
In a woodland where laughter is woven with fun.

As night drapes its blanket, cozy and snug,
The woods hum a tune, inviting a hug.
Close your eyes, dear friend, let your dreams soar,
In this leafy laughter, there's always more!

The Mischief of Moonlit Creatures

Under the moon, a mischief unfolds,
With rabbits in masks, and stories retold.
A dance of shadows, quick on their feet,
As squirrels play tag, what a raucous feat!

The owls spin tales with a wink of their eye,
While badgers toast marshmallows up high.
A hedge full of whispers, where secrets reside,
In this moonlit magic that all critters glide.

Raccoons flip pancakes, a breakfast surprise,
While grasshoppers juggle in moonlit skies.
With laughter that sparkles like stars up above,
These creatures are bound by the warmth of their love.

So, if in the night you hear rapturous cheers,
Know it's the woods playing tricks in your ears.
For in every corner where moonlight will creep,
A party's unfolding, too wild for sleep!

A Jester's Journey

In the forest so green, a jester pranced,
With a cap of bright colors, he twirled and danced.
He juggled with acorns and sang to the trees,
While squirrels dropped branches, just to tickle the breeze.

A frog held a sign that said 'Join the fun!',
While rabbits in bow ties raced under the sun.
They played leapfrog with mushrooms that grew in a row,

As the wind blew the laughter, in waves it did flow.

The grumpy old owl blinked, trying to sleep,
But the jokes were too silly; they made him leap!
He hooted with glee, though he tried to be mad,
This merry parade made him feel oh so glad.

At dusk, with a flourish, the jester took flight,
He danced with the shadows, a whimsical sight.
Though the sun had set low, the fun never ceased,
For joy in the woods brought a laugh-filled feast.

Serendipitous Shadows

Beneath the tall trees where the sunlight would sway,
Giggles of goblins led curious play.
They poked in the bushes, they danced on the logs,
With wands made of twigs and capes made of frogs.

A squirrel in spectacles planned grand events,
While chipmunks in costumes gave regal announcements.

They all gathered 'round for a silly parade,
Where marshmallows flew, and laughter cascaded.

The shadows would change, as the sun started sinking,
With echoes of chuckles in the cool air, blinking.
A hedgehog went roller-skating, quite absurd,
While the critters all chattered, they agreed on the word.

As night fell around, with stars twinkling bright,
They feasted on fireflies that lit up the night.
In the heart of the woods, where silliness thrives,
The magic of laughter kept all of them alive.

The Curious Crickets' Chorus

At twilight, the crickets began a grand show,
With violins fashioned from blades they would blow.
Their tiny legs tapping, creating a beat,
While ants in tuxedos tapped shoes on their feet.

A snail with a mustache claimed he was a star,
While beetles in bowler hats played on guitars.
They all sang together, a whimsical tune,
Underneath the great orb of the glimmering moon.

A hedgehog in shades danced with flair and delight,
While the wise old raccoon critiqued from his height.
He waved a small banner, declaring this night,
'We'll dance till we faint, till the morning's first light!'

As laughter surrounded, the forest came alive,
With jubilation echoing, spirits did thrive.
For in this great orchestra, friendship would bloom,
In the heart of the night, joy chased away gloom.

Jigs of the Juniper

In the dappled glade where the juniper sways,
A troupe of twinkle-folk dance through their days.
With hats made of petals and shoes made of dew,
They prance and they sidestep, all merry and new.

The pine trees were bopping, keeping the beat,
While fairies on fireflies took wing, oh so sweet.
They spun in the breezes and sang with delight,
As the tallest of mushrooms joined in the flight.

A lumbering bear took a turn on the floor,
His two left feet made the crowd call for more.
With a jig and a laugh, he stole the whole show,
As the critters all cheered with a raucous 'ho-ho!'

Come twilight, they gathered for stories and dreams,
Of magical moments and laughter, it seems.
In the jigs of the juniper, joy found its way,
Through silliness woven in dance night and day.

A Stroll Through Dappled Dreams

In shadows where the sunbeams play,
The squirrels dance, in bright array.
With acorn hats on tiny heads,
They crack their jokes and leap from beds.

The flowers giggle, sway, and twist,
In colors no one could resist.
A butterfly with polka dots,
Flutters by, tying up knotted thoughts.

A breeze so cheeky, it will tease,
The branches shake, the leaves appease.
And every step, a secret found,
In this playground, joy abounds.

So take a stroll, let laughter flow,
Where dreams are bright and spirits glow.
In dappled paths of leafy greens,
Adventure waits in silly scenes.

The Mischief of Moss

Beneath the trees, a carpet grows,
A cheeky moss that laughs and knows.
It tickles toes of those who tread,
Jumping up to land on heads!

A friendly toad sits by and grins,
His belly shakes as laughter spins.
He croaks a tune, a jolly beat,
As squirrels join in, tapping feet.

This leafy green, a prankster's space,
Where germs of giggles interlace.
Every step, a jest unfurls,
In nature's theater, magic swirls.

With every bounce, the ferns reply,
As butterflies and bees fly by.
In this mischief, hearts will sing,
With mossy jokes, the woods take wing.

Frothy Streams of Laughter

A brook that bubbles, laughs all day,
With fish that splash, in merry play.
It tickles rocks, a giggling spree,
Where frogs and ducks join in with glee.

Ripples form in silly shapes,
As water skims on its own tapes.
The stones, like grinning faces bright,
Reflect the joy, pure and light.

Oh, how the willows sway and sway,
Encouraging pranks along the way.
They whisper jokes, with rustling leaves,
As shadows dance, the spirit believes.

So come befriend this frothy stream,
Where laughter dances and sparkles beam.
In every splash, a funny scene,
A world of giggles, calm and green.

Frogs in Ties

The frogs all gathered, ties on tight,
In evening's glow, a splendid sight.
With bulging eyes, they take a stand,
Debating issues, oh so grand!

In their fine suits of vibrant hue,
They croak their plans, a ribbit crew.
Discussing meals, and leaps to take,
While dreaming of a grand high stake.

One frog proposes, "Let's have a race!"
All jump in joy, with smiling face.
Hopping past lilies, quick and spry,
The winner claims a pie in the sky!

In this fine bash, they share their jokes,
The night alive with croaks and pokes.
Frogs in ties, with hearts so bright,
In their froggy realm, all feels right.

Jolly Journeys Through Jumbles

In a tangle of twigs, a rabbit wore shoes,
He danced with the squirrels, but sang the blues.
Hiccups from hedgehogs, they tootled and spun,
A party of pines said, "Come join the fun!"

A bear in a bowtie, quite dapper and neat,
Did a jig on his paws to a sweet little beat.
With the frogs as his band, they played on a log,
While the owls hooted softly, "What a fine fog!"

Twirling in circles, a fox tried to trip,
Then slipped on a mushroom, oh what a flip!
The giggles erupted, the forest awake,
As the daisies held hands, the whole world did shake.

And as twilight crept in, with stars all aglow,
The critters fell silent, wrapped in a show.
With laughter still echoing, the night sang its charms,
And the forest kept twinkling with joy in its arms.

Lanterns of the Leafy Lane

Down a path lined with moss, where shadows do play,
The fireflies twinkled, lighting the way.
A turtle in glasses read tales of delight,
While a raccoon juggled with acorns at night.

The whispers of willows shared secrets so sweet,
As chipmunks passed cookies, a very rare treat.
They danced 'round the lanterns, spun round with a cheer,

While the moon teased the stars, "You're not bright, my dear!"

A mushroom wore hats, each one tall and proud,
As they giggled and sighed, all muted and loud.
They painted the night with their colors galore,
While shadows waltzed lightly, craving for more.

So if ever you wander, just follow the light,
Of jolly companions and laughter at night.
In a world spun by magic, that plays on repeat,
You'll find joy in the jumbles, oh what a feat!

The Hummingbird's Prank

A hummingbird zipped with a wink and a smile,
Stealing nectar from blooms, he danced all the while.
He flipped and he flitted, a mischievous sprite,
While flowers all giggled, oh what a sight!

In a splash of sweet color, he darted and dove,
Teasing a bumblebee, "You think you're the grove?"
The bee buzzed back softly, with humor so bright,
"Just wait for a flower, I'll give you a fright!"

The leaves rustled gently, a breeze took the tune,
As the skies watched in wonder, so filled with the moon.
The antics continued, a carnival spree,
And the sun blushed with laughter, "Oh look at me!"

When night finally fell, with stars pure and bold,
The hummingbird chuckled, his stories retold.
In the heart of the garden, where laughter's the plan,
He spun tales of joy, the great prankster man.

Nonsense on the Névé

On a snowy white peak, with a hat made of cheese,
A walrus wore skates, gliding down with ease.
The penguins dressed fancy, all ready to prance,
In the land of the silly, where nobody's glanced.

With snowflakes like confetti, they danced in a line,
While a goat played the flute, said, "Listen, it's fine!"
Beneath icy blue skies, the laughter did echo,
As icicles giggled, hanging like a festo.

A snowman with sunglasses was taking a break,
Sipping hot cocoa from a miniature lake.
He shouted to children, who built him a throne,
"I'm the king of coolness! You ice-up my zone!"

So if you should wander where tumbleweeds freeze,
Join the dance on the névé, a place full of ease.
For laughter is timeless, both silly and sweet,
In the land of the fanciful, where frosty hearts meet.

Treetop Tumblings

Squirrels in hats chase the breeze,
Swinging from branches with utmost ease.
A hedgehog rolls by in a bright red car,
Chasing after a racing star.

The owls are giggling, holding a dance,
While rabbits perform an awkward prance.
A chipmunk in shoes sings a silly tune,
Beneath the bright light of a chuckling moon.

They flip and they tumble, what a sight,
The forest is buzzing with pure delight.
Branches are bouncing, laughter anew,
As nature's odd circus comes into view.

Whimsical Wonders of the Wild

Butterflies play tag with the buzzing bees,
While raccoons juggle acorns with ease.
A deer wears boots, with ribbons and bows,
Dancing on tiptoes as sunlight glows.

The fox pulls a prank with a flick of its tail,
Making the rabbits jump high and scale.
A clever old turtle plays checkers with snails,
And giggles erupt through the winding trails.

Trees whisper secrets, leaves rustle the fun,
As squirrels and mice partake in a run.
Amidst vibrant blossoms in shades that excite,
A world full of wonders sparks joy and delight.

The Fairy's Prancing Trail

On mushrooms with hats, the fairies will glide,
Spinning in circles, with giggles inside.
They twirl through the meadows, on silk-threaded shoes,
Turning the daisies to sparkly hues.

With wands made of wishes, they sprinkle their cheer,
While butterflies flutter from far and near.
A gnome plays the lute, with a grin ear to ear,
His tunes make the flowers sway and appear.

The rabbits join in for a hop-skip parade,
With carrots confetti, the forest's charade.
Picnics and prancing, oh what a delight,
Where laughter rings clear in the soft moonlight.

Ribbons of Radiant Light

Sunlight spills gold through the treetop gates,
As owls throw a party and share silly plates.
The frogs wear caps, sipping dew from a cup,
While dancing on lilypads, never giving up.

A parade of acorns, all five parade,
Adorned in fine jewels no raccoon could trade.
Bouncing and hopping, a toast to the sun,
With every odd critter just having their fun.

With shadows as partners, all steps are just right,
As laughter and giggles make merry the night.
Ribbons of radiant light scattered like dreams,
Where nature's own jesters live out their schemes.

Chronicles of the Wandering Stream

A curious frog in a paper hat,
Waves to a fish, saying, 'Have a chat!'
The turtle forgot, took a swim in the sun,
And the laughter echoed, oh what fun!

A squirrel juggling acorns, quite the show,
While the wise old owl just puts on a glow.
Leaves rustle like giggles, high in the trees,
It's a festival, floating on a breeze!

A message in a bottle, it turns out to be,
A prank from a crab, oh what a spree!
The river winks as it bubbles along,
In this mischievous dream, we all belong.

So come, take a dip in the playful stream,
Where the fish tell stories that make you beam.
A whimsical ride, a giggle-filled race,
Immerse in the joys of this fantastic place.

Beneath a Tapestry of Stars

A raccoon in a tux, quite dapper indeed,
Dancing with fireflies, at night's playful speed.
The moon winks down, with a playful stare,
As the critters all gather for a night fair.

With acorn hats and twinkling lights,
They spin and they twirl under starry sights.
'What if the moon fell?' a hedgehog did muse,
'We'd dance on the ground in our fuzzy shoes!'

Shooting stars race as the frogs start to croak,
Each flicker and flash feels like a good joke.
The laughter erupts as they all take a bow,
Beneath the vast sky, oh, what a wow!

So gather round close, if you're feeling down,
Join in the revels, wear a leaf crown.
For beneath this expanse, where magic holds sway,
Laughter and light chase the worries away.

Marvels in the Mossy Hollow

In a hollow so deep, mushrooms sprout,
Where a snail slid by, squeaking out loud.
A gnome in his garden, quite stubborn and stout,
Yells, 'Why is my radish now looking like a sprout?'

The butterflies giggle, they flutter in glee,
As a pine cone rolls past like it's wild and free.
'What's a critter to do when the sun's all aglow?'
They join in a dance, putting on quite the show!

A ladybug spinning, doing a twist,
As the moss beneath groans, 'Oh, here comes the mist!'
Each droplet that falls, adds rhythm and rhyme,
In this hidden nook, it's a laughter full time.

Where ferns tell their tales in whispers so bold,
And acorns play hide and seek in the gold.
Each creature conspiring for giggles unplanned,
In this merry hollow, just take my hand!

Captured in the Canopy

High up in the branches, a monkey swings round,
Practicing jokes that no one has found.
The parrot caws loud, 'Hey, what's new with you?'
'Just pranks in the treetops,' said the wise kangaroo.

A raccoon on a branch, wearing two left shoes,
Says, 'I may trip, but I won't lose!'
The leaves giggle softly in the twilight's embrace,
While shadows of fun dance in carefree space.

A squirrel with a cape flies high like a dream,
While the wise old owl drops a pun with a beam.
As the night draws near, the stars start to flick,
And laughter still echoes, lighting the trick!

So climb on up high, where the fun never ends,
Beneath a canopy where all nature bends.
With giggles and grins, and joy to unearth,
In this tangle of branches lies all you could thirst.

www.ingramcontent.com/pod-product-compliance
Lightning Source LLC
Chambersburg PA
CBHW051641160426
43209CB00004B/746